The Soldier

THE VIETNAM WAR SOLDIER AT CON THIEN

By Carl R. Green and William R. Sanford

Illustrations by George Martin

Edited by Jean Eggenschwiler
and Kate Nelson

PUBLISHED BY

Capstone Press

Mankato, MN, U.S.A.

Distributed By

𝗖𝗣 CHILDRENS PRESS®
CHICAGO

CIP

LIBRARY OF CONGRESS CATALOGING IN PUBLICATION DATA

Sanford, William R. (William Reynolds), 1927-
The Vietnam War soldier at Con Thien / by William R. Sanford,
Carl R. Green.
p. cm.--(The Soldier)
Summary: Recounts the experiences of an army nurse who served in
Vietnam.
ISBN 1-56065-007-9
1.Vietnamese Conflict, 1961-1975--Juvenile literature. [1.
Vietnamese Conflict, 1961-1975.] I.Green, Carl R. II. Title. III.
Series: Sanford, William R. (William Reynolds), 1927- Soldier.
DS557.7.S36 1989
959.704'3--dc20   **89-25241 CIP AC**

Illustrated by George Martin
Designed by Nathan Y. Jarvis & Associates, Inc.

Capstone Press

Box 669, Mankato, MN, U.S.A. 56001

CONTENTS

THE WAR TO SAVE SOUTH VIETNAM

The Korean War ended in 1953. The communists were not beaten, but the United States did save South Korea's freedom. Americans counted their losses and hoped peace had come to stay. Their hopes were in vain. A new Asian conflict was taking root.

This time Southeast Asia was the trouble spot. After World War II, France had tried to take back its colonies there. The people of Vietnam, led by Ho Chi Minh [hoe chee min], fought back. Ho Chi Minh was a communist. His troops drove out the French in 1954. A treaty divided the region into North and South Vietnam, Laos, and Cambodia. North Vietnam became an ally of

China. South Vietnam allied itself with the U.S.

The plan had been to unite the two Vietnams through free elections. North Vietnam refused. Ho Chi Minh wanted to turn all of Vietnam into a communist state. He began to build up **guerrilla** forces in the south. Known as the Viet Cong, or VC, his men used hit-and-run terror tactics. In 1957 the VC stepped up their attacks against South Vietnam. President Eisenhower sent advisors to train his ally's army. As the Viet Cong grew stronger, more aid was needed. In 1961, President Kennedy sent the first U.S. troops to Vietnam. By 1967 close to half a million men—and women—were on duty there.

Until the 1900s, only men served in the U.S. armed forces. Congress changed that in 1901 by creating the Army Nurse Corps. During World War II, 350,000 women served in the armed forces. They were known as WACS (army), WAVES (navy), and SPARS (Coast Guard). These women nursed the sick and wounded, drove trucks, and ran offices. Although they freed men for combat duty, these women seldom came under fire. In Vietnam, that changed.

Vietnam, Con Thien and the surrounding battle area.

Anita Torres was one of the women who served in Vietnam. Anita grew up in San Antonio, Texas, the oldest of six children. As a teenager, she worked in her father's restaurant. Some of her best customers were nurses from a nearby hospital. Anita began to dream of becoming a nurse, too. Her father liked the idea, but he could not pay for her training. Anita buckled down and earned high grades in junior college. The grades won her a scholarship to nursing school.

The years of training were hard. Anita often said she needed six more hours in the day. Each morning she rode the bus to school. After classes were over she worked as a student nurse. In the evening she waited on tables for two or three hours. Then she hit the books. She often fell asleep while she was reading.

The hard work paid off. Anita won honors as the top student in her class. The entire Torres family stood and cheered the day she was given her nurse's cap.

SOMEONE HAS TO PUT THE GUYS BACK TOGETHER

In 1966 Anita went to work in a hospital emergency room (ER). Night after night she treated the victims of car wrecks, heart attacks, and gang shootings. She learned to stay calm and to think quickly. Later, in her own room, the calm sometimes left her. Those were the times she wept for the patients who could not be saved.

Home was a small house Anita shared with two other nurses. She came home one day to find Betty Collins in the kitchen. Betty waved and poured her a cup of coffee.

"Can you believe it?" Betty said sadly. "Jake and I can't get married after all. He's been **drafted**! After basic training he'll probably be sent to Vietnam. I wish I knew why we're fighting that stupid war."

"Marty Cortez talked about Vietnam while we were dating," Anita said. She missed Marty, who was now on his way to Vietnam. "He said there's no easy way to explain what's going on in 'Nam. Do you want me to try?"

"Sure. Just keep it simple," Betty said.

"The U.S. wants to keep the communists from gobbling up more land," Anita said. "So, it was natural for South Vietnam to ask us for help when the Viet Cong hit them. At the time it looked easy enough. All we had to do was mop up a ragged bunch of guerrillas."

"Why didn't we get the job done?" Betty demanded. "That's where Ho Chi Minh comes in," Anita said. "The North Vietnamese love him because he helped kick the French out. His goal is to turn all of Vietnam into a communist state. To defeat South Vietnam, Ho sends men and guns to the Viet Cong. He says the south will soon be forced to give up."

Betty looked at her watch. "I think I'm starting to get the picture," she said. "Let's talk some more later. I'm on duty in ten minutes."

That night the ER was quiet for once.

Anita had time to watch a newscast. All the scenes seemed to focus on Vietnam. Medics loaded wounded men into helicopters. Viet Cong prisoners stared into the camera. Soldiers ran for cover as rockets blasted an army base.

Then the newscast switched to Washington, D.C. A reporter talked to young men who were burning their draft cards. A crowd marched in front of the White House. People yelled, "Hey, hey, LBJ! How many boys have you killed today?"

"Was President Johnson listening?" Anita asked herself. She hoped not. She did not agree with the antiwar movement. Freedom was worth fighting for, she believed. The words of President Kennedy came back to her. The President had promised that the U.S. would "pay any price, bear any burden, meet any hardship, support any friend, oppose any foe to assure the survival and success of liberty." What price would Anita Torres pay? The wounded soldiers on the screen seemed to reach out to her.

An army recruiter came to the hospital that week. Anita sat down to talk to him. The sergeant told her about the training, the travel, and the adventure of army life. "Nurses don't get hurt," he assured her. "The hospitals are set up in safe areas."

"Save your sales pitch," Anita told him. "I'm joining the army because I want to help my country. Guys are being shot up in Vietnam. I want to be there to patch them up."

A month later, Anita hugged her parents and left for basic training. She felt proud of her shiny second lieutenant's bars. When she reached Fort Sam Houston, the **barracks** were full. Anita and three other nurses were housed in a motel near the base.

"This place is better than a barracks," Anita told her roommates. "Maybe basic training won't be too tough." She changed her mind the next day. The nurses lined up under the stern eye of Captain Fields.

Fields was small, but she had a voice like a foghorn. "It won't be easy, but I'm going to make soldiers out of you," she bellowed.

Like all soldiers, Anita learned to "hurry up and wait." Uniforms came in two sizes, too big and bigger. On the first night she looked at her pile of gear. She was loaded down with a mess kit, helmet, gas mask, canteen, and sleeping bag. She packed it all away and felt more like a soldier. Then she sat down to spit-polish her boots.

At first marching was a bad joke. The drill sergeant kept shouting, "Not that left foot, Lieutenant! Your other left!" Slowly, the lessons took effect. Soon no one was turning right when the sergeant called, "Left face!"

Day by day Anita learned new skills. She fired an **M-16 rifle** and a .45 pistol. She found that map reading was easy. Crawling on her belly under barbed wire was hard. In the mock Vietnamese village she learned more hard lessons. The streets and houses were filled with VC **booby traps**. If she did not fall into a pit lined with bamboo stakes, she might step on a mine.

"Why should I worry about all this?" she wondered. "After all, a nurse's job is to take care of the wounded."

WELCOME TO VIETNAM!

For Anita, the important work began when basic training ended. The nurses' medical training was geared to treating combat **casualties**. They learned to set up a field hospital. Then they took a crash course in operating room procedures. Anita's nights in the ER made that part of the course easier.

The weeks went by quickly. When training was over, Anita went home for a short leave. Then it was time to board an army transport plane bound for 'Nam.

It was a long, tiring flight. After a refueling stop, the plane flew on to South Vietnam. All went well until the 727 began its descent at Tan Son Nhut [tan sun newt] airport. Without warning, the plane swerved to the left. A line of red streaks flashed by Anita's window.

"Those **tracer** bullets nearly got us!" someone shouted.

The pilot spoke on the intercom. "Ol' **Charlie** seems to be a mite upset," he said calmly. "For those of you new to 'Nam, Charlie's short for Victor Charlie, or VC. I vote that we go on to Long Binh [long bin]."

Anita never forgot the sight of those red tracers. In Vietnam, she now knew, everyone was in the front lines.

Long Binh was only a stopover for the nurses. Anita worried about where she would be sent. Some military nurses worked in field hospitals and mobile surgical units. Others cared for the wounded in evacuation hospitals and on hospital ships.

A friendly nurse showed her around. "Sure, it's dangerous here," Kelly said. "But you're needed, believe me. A **GI** starts to get well the instant he sees an American nurse."

Orders came in three days later. Anita was sent to the 3rd Field Hospital in Saigon [sigh-gawn]. Since it was 'Nam's capital city, it sounded safe enough. "Saigon is better than the 'boonies'," Kelly said. "Life is rough in the back country."

16

Anita caught a ride with an army truck. This was her first good look at Vietnam. Water buffalo pulled carts loaded with firewood. Men dressed in loose cotton pants weeded muddy rice paddies. In the villages Anita saw slender women dressed in *ao dais* [ow dyes]. The long dresses of colored silk were slit up the side and worn over white pants. Children lined the road, begging for money. "They almost never smile," the driver said. "All they've got ahead of them is a life of hard work."

The men all seemed to be farmers or soldiers. The farmers looked bent and old. The young soldiers wore GI fatigues, belted tightly around their small waists. "They can't be more than 15 years old," Anita exclaimed.

The war was everywhere. Small villages were circled by coils of barbed wire. Guard towers manned by armed soldiers rose above the straw huts. A warning echoed in Anita's head. "The Viet Cong can attack anywhere at any time," Captain Fields had said. She shuddered and felt better when the truck reached Saigon.

After Anita stowed her gear, the head nurse took her around the hospital. "So the recruiter told you that nurses are safe over here!" Major Louise Adams shook her head. "The fact is, two nurses died in chopper crashes last year. Also, there are snipers and rocket attacks to worry about."

"It's against the rules of war to shoot at hospitals," Anita protested.

Louise laughed. "The VC don't play by the rules. It doesn't matter that you're a nurse. If you're an American, you're a target. Have you met the Vietnamese girl who does our laundry?"

Anita nodded. She had shared a joke with Lai [lie] an hour ago.

"She might be Viet Cong," the major said. "For all we know, she's been telling the VC all about us."

The thought of tiny Lai working for the VC was troubling. Anita changed the subject. "Can't South Vietnam win this war without our help?" she wondered.

The head nurse sounded bitter. "South Vietnam hasn't had a strong leader since 1963," she said. "Since Ngo Dinh Diem [no din dee-EM] was killed, the country has been ruled by generals. Most of them used their power to make money for themselves. Right now General Nguyen Cao Ky [na-wen cow key] is in charge. He's trying to keep the farmers loyal by moving them into safe villages."

"Is the plan working?" Anita asked. "The villagers don't want to leave their own land," Louise said. "Also, the VC promise that things will be better when Ky is overthrown. If I were a simple peasant, I'd be tempted to believe them, too."

LIFE IN A FIELD HOSPITAL

"Here, drink this!" a stern voice ordered.

Anita's vision was blurry. She sipped the cool water and tried to figure out where she was.

"You fainted in the operating room. Haven't you been taking your salt tablets?" the voice said.

Anita blinked and her eyes cleared. She saw Major Wallace bending over her. "Coming from Texas, I thought I knew something about heat," she mumbled. "Here it's always 110 degrees and it feels just as humid. My clothes have mildew and I sweat buckets every day."

"These are the tropics, soldier," the major said. "You should know that you lose body salts when you sweat. Take your salt tablets and you'll be okay."

Anita shared a hut with Gigi Dupont. Gigi took Anita to the officer's club that night. "It's not good to stay in the hut all the time," she warned.

They found a table near a big fan. Anita relaxed a little as some doctors waved to her. "All women feel beautiful here," she said. "The hospital is like that, too. I wear hair ribbons and perfume because the patients like it. At least five of them say they want to marry me."

Gigi studied a bruise on the inside of her arm. "No one will marry me if I have to give any more blood," she complained. "The docs have our blood types posted. When the blood bank runs low, they do their vampire act on us."

Anita left the club early to get some sleep. She was working twelve-hour shifts, six days a week. If the operating room (OR) was busy, she had to stay on duty. Being tired made her nervous. If she slipped up in the OR, a patient might die.

After three months in Saigon, Anita was sent to the 71st Evacuation Hospital at Pleiku [play-koo]. She arrived in October of

1967, just in time for the **monsoon**. The heavy rains sent mud flowing through the hospital's front doors. Mud also oozed up through cracks in the floor of the OR.

At Pleiku, Anita wore her helmet and **flak jacket** at all times. One night, dressing for a party, she was tempted to forget the bulky jacket. Later she was glad she wore it.

The party had just started when a siren wailed. Someone shouted, "Incoming!" Anita dove under a table just as a rocket exploded outside. She looked up to see that some of her friends were still dancing. The old Pleiku hands did not scare easily.

The rocket attack went on for an hour. When the all-clear sounded the party broke up. "How do we know the VC won't attack again?" Anita asked Dr. Ross.

The doctor rubbed his eyes. He had been digging **shrapnel** out of wounded soldiers for three straight days. "Oh, Charlie never hits us twice in a row," he said. "The VC slip into the woods after dark and set up their rockets. Then they attach cheap timers. By the time the rockets go up, they're long gone."

Anita was shaken even more when she reached her hut. A rocket blast had sent a roof beam crashing down on her cot. "What if I hadn't gone to the party?" she asked herself. "I'd have been sitting on that cot writing letters."

To calm down, Anita grabbed a towel and headed for the showers. She was half way to the shower room when a new **barrage** of rockets hit. Instantly, she flopped into a drainage ditch. Ten minutes later the attack was over. As she scraped at the mud, Anita hoped Dr. Ross was deep in a ditch, too.

Each day the nurses saw the harm war does to the body. Anita treated men with bullet wounds, head injuries, burns, and infections. She saw soldiers with fevers rarely seen at home. The most unusual cases were those of bubonic plague. The disease was spread by fleas, of which Vietnam had more than its share.

Each hour seemed to bring a new horror story. Two soldiers came in carrying their buddy. They had made a stretcher of tree branches and jackets. All three were caked with blood and mud. After escaping from the VC they had walked through 50 miles of jungle in their bare feet. Anita had to say "no" when they begged for steak and ice cream. "Get over the **dysentery**," she said. "Then I'll bring you hot fudge sundaes."

The hospital also cared for prisoners and for the local people. Anita hated the VC, but she gave them the best care she could. "That's what nurses do," she told herself. The people were Montagnards [mon-tawn-YARDS], members of a mountain tribe. They wanted only to be left in peace. The VC did not think that way. By torturing Montagnard men they could force the villagers to give them shelter.

A bright moment came the day Anita helped a woman give birth. As she held the tiny infant she thought, "I've seen too much death. It's great to know that life does go on."

A BRIEF TIME-OUT

"Rest and Recuperation! What glorious words!" Anita danced around the hut and threw civilian clothes into a suitcase.

Gigi hummed as she did her own packing. "Five days **R&R** in Hong Kong makes life worth living," she agreed. "We're going to stuff ourselves with Chinese food. Then we'll hit Canton Road to buy some jade for the folks back home."

"Don't forget the horse races in Happy Valley," Anita added. "Best of all, we'll sleep 'til noon. I may not find a place that serves chili, but you can't have it all."

The nurses flew to Hong Kong dressed in their Class A uniforms. Anita thought the green skirt, blouse, and jacket made her look too military. She longed to put on earrings and a soft jersey dress.

Their room in Hong Kong was full of wonders. Gigi bounced on the soft bed and sipped a cool soft drink. Anita ran a hot bath and dumped in a big handful of bubble bath.

Gigi ordered lunch from room service while Anita soaked in the tub. "Sorry, Anita," she called, hanging up the phone with a laugh. "The cook doesn't know how to make tacos. We'll have to make do with ham on rye."

The days went by in a whirl of sightseeing and shopping. Anita bought a roll of silk and had herself measured for a suit. A boy brought the finished suit to the hotel the next day. At night they walked the streets, dazzled by the lights of the great city. The world of rockets, mud, and wounded men seemed far away.

On the sixth day they flew back to Pleiku. Nothing had changed. The VC greeted them with a rocket attack that night. Only the mail from home kept them from weeping.

Anita read her letters three and four times. Her parents also sent news clips and snapshots. She kept the photos in an album.

Family pictures went into a section called "The Real World." A second section was labeled "Never-Never Land." That was for her Vietnam snapshots.

The monthly packages were prizes beyond cost. This month's box held a tube of shampoo, home-baked cookies, and the latest music tapes. The biggest prize of all had been an electric blanket. By leaving the blanket turned on all day, Anita kept the damp out of her sheets.

USO troupes were another tie with home. Film stars, comics, and singers visited the wounded. They came to chat, sign autographs, and put on a show. The shows were instant hits. Badly injured men always cheered up when a pretty girl sang their favorite songs.

Outdoor shows were held around Saigon, but not at Pleiku. There was always the danger that a large crowd might draw a rocket attack. Even the USO troupes were in danger. The VC had hidden a bomb in Bob Hope's hotel in Saigon in 1964. Luckily the star was not there when the bomb went off. Hope got a big laugh that night. He told the troops, "Just as I landed at Tan Son Nhut, I saw a hotel go by."

One of Anita's jobs was to talk to wounded soldiers. Having someone to talk to was part of getting well. It was the GI's who told her about **Agent Orange**.

Sergeant Tusker told her what was going on. "The campaign started in 1961," he told her. "The army calls it '**defoliation**'.

Low-flying planes spray a weed killer onto the forests where the VC hide. The chemical—Agent Orange—causes the trees to lose their leaves. With his cover gone, Charlie can't hide his supply lines from our bombers."

"Do we only spray their supply lines?" Anita wondered.

"We spray wherever there are Viet Cong," Tusker said. He paused and moved his injured leg. "In the Mekong [may-kong] River delta we've sprayed manioc [MAN-e-ock] trees," he went on. "That keeps the VC from using the roots for food."

"What if the spray lands on a farmer's fields?" Anita asked.

"If our planes hit a rice paddy, the rice dies," Tusker said. "As the bumper stickers say, 'War is bad for all living things.' Using the spray makes sense only if it ends the war sooner."

Anita thought of a new worry. "The soldiers think that Agent Orange harms people, too," she said.

"I'm no chemist," Tusker told her, "but I did read up on weed killers. The main chemical in Agent Orange is dioxin [die-OK-sin]. In high doses it affects the skin, liver, and nervous system. There's a chance it can cause cancer and birth defects. Believe me, our guys handle it with care. Even so, some of our troops have been sprayed by mistake."

Like so much else in Vietnam, the question nagged at Anita. Was it okay to use any means to win a war? Was Agent Orange any worse than the poisoned bamboo stakes in a VC booby trap? "All wars are crazy," she decided. "Vietnam is just a little more so."

THE BATTLE OF CON THIEN

"Come up and see me," the letter ended. Anita smiled at the thought of seeing Betty Collins again. Betty was serving in a field hospital near the Demilitarized Zone (**DMZ**).

The DMZ was near the 17th parallel, the dividing line between the two Vietnams. There was plenty of action up there. General Westmoreland, the U.S. commander, had sent Marines to defend the area. One of their jobs was to cut the VC's supply lines.

Anita asked for a weekend pass. Then she hitched a chopper ride up north. When she met Betty, her friend snapped a salute.

"You're a first lieutenant now!" Betty said.

Anita laughed and touched her silver

bar. "Show me around," she ordered with a mock growl.

Betty pointed to a line of huts and tents. "It's not much, but it looks good to a wounded Marine," she said. "Now, come sit in on our weekly briefing."

A major was rattling off the gloomy facts. "By the end of 1967 we'll have half a million troops in Vietnam. But the VC are like the fairy tale snake. They grow two new heads as soon as we chop one off. We've cut their supply trails through the DMZ. Now they're using the Ho Chi Minh Trail through Laos and Cambodia. That's off limits to our bombers."

"Why don't we invade North Vietnam and win this war?" Anita muttered. She knew the answer. Both the Soviet Union and China were helping North Vietnam. In 1950 U.S. troops had come close to the Chinese border during the Korean War. That brought Chinese troops into the war to fight beside the North Koreans. Their entry kept the war going. After that, the lesson was clear. An invasion of North Vietnam might mean a second war with China. No one wanted to wake that sleeping giant.

"It's a no-win game," Anita whispered

to Betty. "Our guys are fighting a war they aren't allowed to win."

Later that day the two nurses flew in a **med-evac helicopter** to Con Thien [kon thee-en]. The Marine base was on a low, muddy hill two miles from the DMZ. The sea was 14 miles away. Each strong point was ringed by barbed wire, mines, and shell craters. As the chopper circled, Anita could see **bunkers** lined with sandbags. The Marines lived in those dugouts.

"Half of our casualties come from shell and rocket barrages," Betty said. "Lately we've been treating men who are shell shocked by the constant shelling. A shell shock case is out of action just as if he'd been wounded. What's more, that's not the VC shooting at us up here. Our guys are facing four divisions of North Vietnam's best troops."

"At least there's a front line," Anita said. "We know where the enemy is dug in. Can't our bombers wipe them out?"

Betty shook her head. "They've tried. A major told me the air force has dropped 42 million pounds of bombs. Our big guns have fired 700,000 rounds. Navy ships have lobbed in another 50,000 shells. The North Vietnamese just dig deeper and shoot back. In one day the 9th Marines lost 300 men not far from here."

"It's really strange," Betty said as the chopper landed. "In Vietnamese, Con Thien means 'Hill of the Angels'."

The chopper's rotors were still turning when the first incoming shell hit. "Head for the bunker, on the double!" the pilot yelled. The two nurses ran for shelter, held up only by a line of ammo trucks. A second shell exploded, spraying the landing zone with mud and shrapnel. At last, mud-spattered and panting, they reached the bunker.

"Good morning," a cheery Marine captain greeted them. He did not seem to notice the shelling. "I saw you dodging those trucks. Were any of them pulling water trailers? If not, we'll miss our showers again."

"I was too busy keeping my head down," Anita answered. "What would happen if a shell hit one of those ammo trucks?"

The captain grinned. "Why, it would have been like a second Fourth of July, that's all." Just then a rat scurried across the floor. As the nurses jumped back, a second Marine grabbed a slingshot. His well-aimed rock thunked the rat in the head and killed it.

"Sorry about the noisy welcome," the

34

captain said. "As soon as the barrage stops I'll take you to the **sick bay**. The boys have been looking forward to your visit."

The sick bay was set up inside a crude bunker. Anita counted eight patients in the small room. She helped Betty check the bottles that dripped fluids into veins. Then they changed blood-soaked dressings. The men with the worst wounds would be flown out first. "The helicopters are priceless," Anita thought. "A long, bumpy ride in a truck could kill these guys."

THE LIGHT AT THE END OF THE TUNNEL

The army sent Anita and Gigi back to Saigon in January, 1968. Dreams of Con Thien were still haunting Anita's sleep. She waved a news magazine. "Look at this," she said to Gigi. "Some of our leaders think we're winning this war. They're saying, 'There's a light at the end of the tunnel'."

Gigi pretended to peer down a long tunnel. "I do see a light at the end," she said, sounding amazed. "Oh, sorry about that. It's not a victory bonfire. It's a burning supply dump."

The nurses had looked forward to a few peaceful days. Both sides always called a cease-fire during the new year's holiday called **Tet** [rhymes with pet]. This year the North Vietnamese made other plans. They knew the battles around Con Thien were keeping U.S. forces busy. Before dawn on January 31 the VC switched targets. Charlie attacked South Vietnam's cities.

Anita awoke to the sound of heavy firing. Helicopter gunships were circling overhead. A **sniper's** bullet pinged off her hut as she pulled on her flak jacket. Outside, the sky was turning red with flames. For a moment she thought all of Tan Son Nhut airfield was ablaze. Fearing the worst, Anita sprinted for the hospital.

The wounded were there ahead of her. Anita went down the line of stretchers, checking each man. There were hard choices to make. Medicines, blood plasma, and space in the ORs were running short. The doctors gave priority to the men with the best chance of surviving.

Someone said the VC had broken into the U.S. embassy. What if they attacked the hospital? Anita looked at the M-16 rifles stacked by the wall. Could she shoot a Viet Cong? "To save these wounded men," she told herself, "I'll do what I have to do."

The hospital was in the middle of a war zone now. Medics carried in a GI with a rifle **grenade** embedded in his stomach. The staff had to pile sandbags around him before a doctor could go to work. Everyone clapped when the grenade came out. A bomb squad took the grenade away.

A row of Viet Cong bodies lay near the hospital. Some of them were women. "That's rough," Anita thought, "but it works both ways." A group of U.S. women had been cut down by rifle fire near the officers' club. As Anita cleaned her wounds, a young Red Cross worker described the scene.

"Charlie was camped on a telephone pole outside the fence," she said. "He got us, but he missed a better target. Ten air force generals were hunkered down less than 50 feet away."

Late that night Anita went to a warehouse for bandages. She was almost back at the hospital when a guard yelled, "Halt!" Before she could answer, she heard a loud click. The guard had released the safety catch on his rifle.

"It's okay, I'm a nurse," she called.

The guard stepped forward and looked her over. "All right, go ahead," he said. "We have to be careful. Some VC tried to sneak onto the base dressed in GI uniforms."

After 30 hours on her feet, Anita was told she could take a break. She dragged a mattress into a supply room and fell asleep at once. Fifteen minutes later she was shaken awake. "Incoming wounded," Major Wallace told her. "We've got more work to do."

The weeks after Tet crept by. Anita's one-year tour of duty was coming to an end. "I'm not the same person who arrived here a year ago," she told herself. "War changes people. I feel a lot older and maybe a little wiser."

She did not try to explain her feelings to her parents. She did send them a copy of a letter the nurses were passing around. It used humor to hint at the affect of the war. The letter read:

"Dear Friends and Loved Ones:

"This gal is coming home from a year in Vietnam. Here's how you can help her. The first few times she rides in your car, remind her to shut the door. Jeeps don't have doors. Stop her if she puts her feet on the dashboard. If she tries to stand in line for supper, guide her to a chair.

"She may put blankets, flashlights, and

books under her bed. That's because she isn't certain your house won't be shelled. If you make a sudden loud noise, she'll probably dive to the floor.

"Be patient. It takes a while to adjust to the real world."

The day came when Anita said goodbye to her friends. To her relief, the plane took off without a goodbye rocket from Charlie. Vietnam was soon a distant smudge on the horizon.

"It's strange," Anita thought. "I feel happy to be going home. Yet I feel sad, too. There's still so much work to do in Vietnam. I wonder if we'll ever defeat the Viet Cong?"

AFTER THE BATTLE

Anita came home to a nation that now hated the war. This feeling turned the 1968 election upside down. An antiwar candidate almost upset President Lyndon Johnson in the New Hampshire primary. The close call led Johnson to announce that he would not run for a second full term. The Republicans named Richard Nixon to run for the White House. Nixon promised to build up the South Vietnamese army. Once that was done, he said, he would bring our boys home. He won the fall election.

The U.S. was ready to make peace, but the North Vietnamese refused. They said they would talk only if U.S. troops left the south. President Nixon refused. He ordered the air force to bomb North Vietnam. He also sent troops into Cambodia to cut Viet Cong supply lines. Months later, the pressure led North Vietnam to the peace table.

The two sides agreed on terms in early 1973. The treaty called for a cease-fire and the withdrawal of U.S. troops. The Americans pulled out, but the communists soon broke the cease-fire. The weary South Vietnamese tried to fight, but the communists were too strong. Guns and supplies from the U.S. were not enough to save South Vietnam. On April 30, 1975 North Vietnamese troops marched into Saigon. Almost 60,000 U.S. soldiers had died in a lost cause.

The pictures of the fall of Saigon brought tears to Anita's eyes. By then she was no longer an army nurse. She had resigned in 1971 because she did not enjoy peacetime nursing. In Vietnam she had been treated as a near-equal by the doctors. Now she had to stand by and watch doctors do work she could do better. Anita also saw that the veterans of 'Nam needed more than medical care. Many of them came home with emotional problems.

Anita went back to college and majored in psychology. With her degree in hand, she found work as a counselor. Healing minds was harder than healing bodies. A few of her patients had to be sent to mental hospitals. Two took their own lives.

The failures hurt, but Anita had successes, too. A Texas rancher named Wesley Starr was one of them. Wes and Anita were married soon after he left the clinic. Today, Anita still counsels on a part-time basis. Most of her energy goes into raising her two children.

For Anita Torres Starr, Vietnam seems long ago and far away. Once in a while she dreams of rocket attacks and long rows of wounded GIs. Those are the nights she wakes up with her heart pounding. It is always an hour or more before she can go back to sleep.

GLOSSARY

Important Historic Figures

HO CHI MINH (1890-1969)—The Communist leader of North Vietnam. He supported the Viet Cong guerrillas in their battle to overthrow the government of South Vietnam.

PRESIDENT LYNDON JOHNSON (1908-1973)—36th President of the United States. Johnson was President during the greatest buildup of U.S. forces in Vietnam.

PRESIDENT JOHN KENNEDY (1917-1963)—35th President of the United States. Kennedy was the President who sent the first U.S. combat troops to Vietnam.

PRESIDENT RICHARD NIXON (1913-)—37th President of the United States. Nixon withdrew U.S. troops after a cease-fire was signed. The Communists later broke the cease-fire and overran South Vietnam.

GENERAL WILLIAM WESTMORELAND (1914-)— Commanding general of U.S. troops in Vietnam.

44

Important Terms

AGENT ORANGE—A powerful weed killer that was sprayed on the forests that hid Communist supply lines in Vietnam.

BARRACKS—A building (or buildings) used to house soldiers.

BARRAGE—A heavy, sustained volume of artillery fire.

BOOBY TRAP—An apparently harmless device that is designed to injure any soldier who touches it.

BUNKER—A fortified earthwork, often reinforced with timbers and sandbags.

CASUALTIES—Soldiers who are killed or wounded in action.

CHARLIE—GI slang for a member of the Viet Cong.

DEFOLIATION—The process of killing vegetation in order to reveal enemy camps and supply lines.

DMZ—The Demilitarized Zone between North and South Vietnam. The zone was meant to provide a buffer between the two countries.

DRAFT—The forced selection of people for military service.

DYSENTERY—An infection of the lower intestines that causes pain, fever, and diarrhea.

FLAK JACKET—A sleeveless armored vest that soldiers wear to protect them from enemy fire.

GI—A slang term for an American soldier. GI stands for "government issue," a term applied to anything provided by the army's supply department.

GRENADE—A small bomb meant to be thrown by hand or fired from a specially equipped rifle.

GUERRILLAS—Small, mobile military forces that specialize in hit-and-run attacks. Guerrillas try to blend in with the local people while operating in enemy territory.

MED-EVAC HELICOPTER—A helicopter equipped to pick up wounded soldiers for quick delivery to a hospital.

MONSOON—A wind system that brings heavy rains during the wet season in Southeast Asia.

M-16 RIFLE—The standard infantry rifle of the Vietnam War. The 5.56-mm M-16 was capable of single shot or automatic fire. On full automatic it fired at a rate of about 700 rounds per minute. The rifle was not popular with the GIs because it often jammed.

R&R—Army slang for Rest and Recuperation leave. R&R gives soldiers a chance to recover from the hardships of life in a combat zone.

SHRAPNEL—Sharp metal fragments hurled through the air by the explosion of an artillery shell.

SICK BAY—Marine term for a hospital or first aid station.

SNIPER—A sharpshooter who fires from a concealed position.

TET—The Vietnamese New Year's holiday.

TRACER—A bullet that leaves a glowing, smokey trail along its path. Soldiers use tracers to correct their aim once they know where their bullets are going.

USO (UNITED SERVICE ORGANIZATION)—The organization that provided entertainment for the troops in Vietnam.

959.704   Sanford, William R
San
     The Vietnam War
     soldier at Con
     Thien

LOCKHART ELEMENTARY SCHOOL

 GUMDROP BOOKS - Bethany, Missouri